The World Needs Marriage Equality Now

A collection of articles about marriage equality,

Written in 2011-2013,

By TaraElla

Table of Contents

Understanding the Implications

How Many People are Affected by Marriage Equality?

I'd Rather Burn in Hell than Support Bigotry

How Marriage Equality Will Save Marriage and Families

We all need to recognise one thing: marriage is in crisis. Marriage rates have been declining for many years, and the decline has not halted unfortunately. If the trend is not reversed, I am afraid that many of us will live to see a time when marriage will have become a minority concern. It's a tough reality, but it's one that we need to face.

In response to this phenomenon, there have been efforts on marriage promotion. However, these have been very limited in their success. Just why marriage promotion is not working very well needs to be studied, and programs will need to be improved upon. I suspect that opponents painting marriage as outdated, hierarchical and elitist, amongst other things, have had at least some effect. I don't believe in any of that rubbish personally, but I know people who do. In the long run we need strategies to defeat comprehensively the 'liberation' ideology that has torpedoed marriage. However, there is no way we can win either the short or long term game on this without marriage equality.

Looking into the future, there is one clear threat to marriage promotion: that much of the younger generation are starting to see marriage as an exclusionary, bigoted institution. In fact, it is happening right now - there have been plenty of reports of young people including pleas for marriage equality in their ceremonies, feeling conflicted about sending out the marriage invites, etc. Not every young couple feels the same disgust about the exclusionary aspects, but as long as a significant proportion of the younger generation do feel this way, I suspect few of them would be too happy to get on board marriage promotion or be actively pro-marriage in culture. Not when it is promoting an institution excluding and hurting their gay and lesbian friends, and in many cases, family members.

Let me put it more bluntly: when marriage clearly excludes gay and lesbian couples, every word of marriage promotion will hurt their feelings - this is literally true, and something that cannot be said any milder. As a result, marriage promotion will rightly be seen as a hurtful exercise by many young people. Even I, a supporter of marriage, have had trouble explaining to my friends that whilst I support marriage I don't support the exclusionary aspect of the marriage laws out there. I simply have given up on talking about the matter most of the time.

Most of the older generations will have a difficult time grasping the concepts outlined above. After all, their generation of gay people are often more closeted, and many were/are not that interested in marriage. In any case, the older generations developed their attitudes towards marriage without the same sex marriage issue in consideration. However, they must try to put themselves in the shoes of the younger generations if marriage revitalisation and promotion is to work in the younger generations. After all, the most important place for marriage to flourish, the most important cohort for which marriage must remain strong, is the younger generations - because they are or soon will be raising the next generation.

Just like on many other issues, standing still and not changing a thing does not mean we can go back to the past. It does not mean conservative values won't miss out. Inaction is dangerous, especially when the world is changing. If a significant portion of a whole generation becomes ambivalent to marriage, the damage may take many generations to repair. On the other hand, if we take advantage of the opportunity of marriage equality and usher in a new era of public conversation and enthusiasm about marriage, things won't change overnight, but over time they will, in the direction we want things to change. And whilst political issues often take a long time to resolve, ten years down the line it may already be too late to grasp this opportunity. Now is the time to support marriage equality, for anyone who is serious about the future of marriage and family values in society.

Answering Some Arguments Against Marriage Equality

1. Gay marriages destroy the purpose of procreation in marriage, and leads to the destruction of the 'conjugal' and 'fruitful' reasons for marriage.

If we are to be strict about this, any proven infertile couple should be excluded too. However, that would taint marriage as a harsh and exclusionary institution, and in an age where it has become an option rather than a necessity, would drive many away from it. In the eyes of many particularly younger people, excluding gay couples is just as cruel. Again, rigidity should not apply. We can still strongly stress that marriage is for procreation as a primary purpose, whilst still stressing that we need to be inclusive and compassionate otherwise, and therefore cannot use black-and-white rules to shut people out. This isn't too hard to understand, is it?

2. Marriage is meant to be a complimentary institution.

This is a useful concept, but a really wishy-washy rule. Not all opposite sex couples are complimentary in their character, and certainly not all opposite sex couples are complimentary in a particular way that same sex couples cannot be, unless you are talking about the physical only.

If physical complementariness is what you're talking about, many infertile couples should be excluded too, as should couples were one member was born with certain 'intersex' medical conditions (e.g. Klinefelter's syndrome - look it up if you don't know what it is), as they are not strictly complementary either. The trouble is that, many men with Klinefelter's don't even know they have it! Again, complementariness is often the case, but we cannot be rigid here.

If spiritual complementariness is what you're talking about, many straight couples come together because of similarity rather than complementariness (think many geeky couples), or because they are complimentary in non-traditional ways (e.g. the alpha female and the omega male), and these have clear parallels in same sex couples too. Of course most people still live out traditional gender roles and always will. But society has already decided that non-traditional gender roles are OK too for the minority whose lives are like that - and as long as they are heterosexual they can legally marry too. Therefore, if those people are allowed to marry legally, why not same sex couples?

3. Gay Couples are Not the Same Thing as Straight Couples

This tends to not be very convincing for those who know gay couples well, again more commonly found in the younger generation. Therefore, this argument is often voiced and accepted by older opponents of equality. And for good reason too - for those who have observed and known gay couples, they will find that there isn't a clear line they can draw, except regarding physical body parts.

Different straight couples bond over different things or reasons, and their relationships are held together by very different central concepts. Technically, they can be divided into different categories too. In this sense maybe we can have the glamour-marriage, the religious-marriage, the Chinese-marriage, the Irish-marriage and so on. But we don't do that - marriage is a broad church and a society wide brand, and for a good reason. On the other hand, one straight couple's relationship may have more in common with a same sex couple's relationship than with another straight couple, other than the body parts. So it doesn't make sense to draw the line at the body parts thing, right?

4. It has Historically Been This Way

There was much confusion and ignorance around same sex attracted people in history. They were just not allowed to live openly as couples. Now that this is no longer the case, not only is denial of legal marriage ridiculous and arbitrary, it threatens to delegitimize marriage in an age where already it is seen as 'only a choice'. In fact, that some couples can be allowed to live openly in relationships but not to be married is entirely the creation of the 'liberation' of the 70s and 80s anyway. As conservatives, we should not just allow marriage equality, but we should encourage gay couples to get married, like society encouraged everyone living in a couple relationship to get married bak when family values were strong. Marriage equality presents a chance to re-assert pre-liberation culture.

5. The Family has been destroyed enough in the 20th century

This had nothing to do with gay people, and it was all due to 'liberation ideology', which marriage equality does not come from and is often diametrically opposed to. Many marriage equality supporters are opposed to 'liberation ideology' in almost every form. It is also inconceivable that marriage equality would lead to any change in most marriages, the way that no fault divorce changed the landscape for example. No fault divorce applied to every single marriage, whilst same sex marriages do not change a thing about any heterosexual marriage.

In fact, for marriage promotion to work and to have a strong case against liberation ideology, we need to show everyone that traditional values are to be aspired for, can be aspired to by everybody, and are not bigoted or apartheid-supporting. When there is a consensus about gay people not being able to change their sexual orientation, if marriage excludes gay people it will always be seen as bigoted and apartheid supporting by a large proportion of the younger population.

6. It Defeats the State's Purpose of Benefiting Marriage

If we think of the purpose of marriage in society narrowly, the state also should not benefit any infertile and childless marriages. However, part of the way marriage works is by upholding marriage as a brand for the whole society, and that brand needs to be inclusive and non-bigoted to have the most appeal to potential supporters for it to work that way. The benefits of this will return to the majority of marriages – i.e. child bearing, fertile heterosexual marriages, by encouraging marriage and a strong marriage culture in the whole population. Hence same sex marriages still support the state's purpose of benefitting marriage, although more indirectly. Moreover, further benefits can be seen in a general return to commitment and family values, reduction of STI and HIV rates in certain communities, etc.

7. It Imposes Its Acceptance on All Society

This is a myth. See the Canadian Civil Marriage Act 2005 and what it says, for example. When a law is written that way, to impose its acceptance on all society would require ANOTHER change in law, which may even be unconstitutional in most countries.

On the other hand, opponents of marriage equality are forcing THEIR version of marriage down the throats of everybody else, by having it enshrined in national law. It doesn't matter than theirs is the traditional version - it is no longer accepted as a consensus in most of the West either, and is thought of as offensive by many people in our society.

When there is a clear conflict between two visions of a shared thing (our laws), we should proceed to consider the most inclusive solution. As the equal definition of marriage also includes all heterosexual marriages, but the heterosexual definition excludes same sex marriages, society should opt for the more inclusive definition, which would satisfy to a degree everyone on both sides, as nobody's actual rights get compromised.

Reports about businesses being 'forced' to serve gay couples have not been due to marriage laws. In fact, many such reports have come from Australia, the UK and many other countries where marriage equality is not yet the law. It has to do with the anti-discrimination law in these countries, which often say that businesses must not serve gay people, and by extension gay couples, any differently to the way they serve straight people. Marriage does not appear to factor into this.

Marriage Equality: A Case of Gays Saying 'Look At Me Now'?

To many observers, gay couples campaigning to be included in marriage seems like yet another 'Look At Me Now' moment. We have long repealed any laws against gay behaviour, we have given them couple rights in society, in many places we have given them the option of civil unions, and yet they are screaming for more. Aren't we fed up by now? Won't they take what they have and go away quietly?

Once upon a time I thought like that too. Then I studied the topic carefully, and I found out just how wrong I was.

The gay and lesbian couples seeking marriage and a family life, even if they do not have children to raise, are actively seeking to join the age old tradition of marriage and commitment. They have actively rejected the 'liberation' movement, which has promised them a life of endless hedonism, lots of sexual freedom and no institutions to rule their lives by. Just like us, they have chosen to reject the postmodern promise of endless freedom and have chosen to embrace instead the tradition of commitment and family values. Not many people out there are aware of this, but for choosing to side with tradition they often face the ridicule, disdain and outright discouragement of more 'liberation' orientated gay and lesbian people. For choosing to adopt our values and join our lifestyle, they have been derided as asssimilationists, people who are ashamed of who they are and seek conservative society's approval at all costs. We, the people who embrace family values, are their natural home. To reject them here too would be far too cruel and indeed inconsistent with our compassionate family values. To reject them would also be to confirm that their critics are right, that being gay means you cannot embrace family values, that you must embrace 'liberationism'. I really don't think that is the right message to send.

The fact that gay and lesbian couples are actively rejecting 'liberation' and embracing the tradition of marriage is another thing we should take heart to, and may even be able to use as a starting point for a general return to family values in society. The fact that gay and lesbian couples, who live in a culture where just a decade or so ago 'liberation' was the norm, have come to reject it so decisively, can be a great conversation starter for a wider societal discussion on marriage and family values, and why they represent a superior lifestyle to 'liberation'. Again, it is an opportunity we can only take if we first embrace the idea of marriage equality first.

A related argument is that gay marriages will never be universally accepted as real marriages, not by many churches at least. So why should they bother? Well, I personally still see an ideal for the future where divorce rates go back down to 1950s levels for all couples - again this is not universally accepted as a goal. Shall we just give up on everything then? I guess not. If it's good for family values in the end, we should embrace it. Others may take a longer time to do so, but we should be part of the process to help along any idea that may bolster family values for our future generations. Letting go of this (or any other) opportunity is not something we can afford to do, when the future of family values is already looking this shaky.

What Marriage Really Is, and How it Relates to Marriage Equality

One major concern of modern times is that marriage rates have declined, generation after generation. Non-marriage births have risen all over the West. Another concern with marriage right now is the sky high divorce rates. A society with divorce rates above 40% really is not sustainable in the long run, I believe.

The proposed solution is to restart a conversation about what marriage is and what the commitment means. Remake the case about marriage, procreation and family - specifically how marriage is a commitment that is not just about the 'love' and desires of adults, but rather a stabilising institution that forms a good foundation for a family. I totally agree that this would help a lot. As a society, we should discuss and hopefully come to a conclusion that marriage is not just about love or adult desires, but is about the formation of families and providing for them a stable structure.

Some people have suggested that including gay couples in marriage would take us further away from the above consensus. In fact, some have even suggested that it is because society has lost the above consensus regarding marriage that the idea of gay marriages has become appealing to young people in society. I disagree with all of this. In fact, I not only disagree with all of this, but I will take the opposite view: embracing marriage equality is the first step in having the public conversation about marriage, in getting the public to be receptive of our arguments, and the only way in which a consensus about the nature of marriage can be re-established.

Honestly, if the arguments about marriage, procreation and stable families are tied to necessarily excluding gay couples, it wouldn't work. It would severely turn off at least a significant proportion of society - many of which will be young people, the very people who the conversation ought to engage to be successful. Many young people now believe that excluding gay and lesbian couples from marriage is unacceptable, period. Through these lens, any argument purporting to make a case to exclude gay people from marriage will be seen as bigoted.

I propose an alternative: we need to allow gay and lesbian couples to get married as a matter of equal compassion and inclusion. Once this issue is sorted out, the clean air then lets us deal with the matter of what marriage is. No longer will idea about marriage, procreation and stable families be associated with bigotry. My critics say that including gay couples necessarily defeats the procreation and family idea of marriage. I strongly disagree. We already do include infertile and childless couples in marriage - as a society, we have long believed excluding them will be too cruel an act, whilst including them will not affect the function and ideal of the majority of procreating marriages and families. Whilst the older generation may be used to the idea of marriage excluding gay couples, for much of the younger generation, their exclusion is just as cruel as excluding infertile couples. Including gay and lesbian couples, who are by definition infertile couples, would not really distract from the idea of marriage being for procreation and for the stability of families resulting from the procreation act, any more than allowing heterosexual childless or infertile couples to marry (as we currently do) would. In reality, being rigid rarely works. I believe it would make perfect sense to say that marriage was meant to help couples set up family by encouraging procreation and then providing a stable structure for the resulting family, but being an inclusive society, we also extend this institution to cover those couples who unfortunately cannot procreate but are living in similarly committed arrangements.

The Conservative Case for Marriage Equality

By the time this is being written, there are many articles entitled 'The Conservative Case for Marriage Equality', written by many people. The points are now well established and repeated again and again by now. I am not going over all of those points again. I am going to provide a fresh perspective on the matter: my own perspective, from my deep study in recent years into the topic.

I want to talk about marriage itself first. We all need to recognise one thing: marriage is in crisis. Marriage rates have been declining for many years, and the decline has not halted unfortunately. If the trend is not reversed, I am afraid that many of us will live to see a time when marriage will have become a minority concern. It's a tough reality, but it's one that we need to face. In response to this phenomenon, there have been efforts on marriage promotion. However, these have been very limited in their success. Still, we keep doing it because it's the only hope to keep marriage alive. Just why marriage promotion is not working very well needs to be studied, and programs will need to be improved upon. I suspect that opponents painting marriage as outdated, hierarchical and elitist, amongst other things, have had at least some effect. I don't believe in any of that rubbish personally, but I know people who do. In the long run we need strategies to defeat comprehensively the 'liberation' ideology that has torpedoed marriage.

However, right now, perhaps more urgently, there is one clear threat to marriage promotion: that much of the younger generation are starting to see marriage as an exclusionary, bigoted institution. And whilst that may not mean they will all refuse to get married, I suspect few of them would be too happy to get on board marriage promotion when it is promoting an institution excluding and hurting their gay and lesbian friends, and in many cases, family members. When marriage clearly excludes gay and lesbian couples, every word of marriage promotion will hurt their feelings - this is literally true, and something that cannot be said any milder. As a result, marriage promotion will rightly be seen as a hurtful exercise by many young people. Even I, a supporter of marriage, have had trouble explaining to my friends that whilst I support marriage I don't support the exclusionary aspect of the marriage laws out there. I simply have given up on talking about the matter most of the time.

Another concern with marriage right now is the sky high divorce rates. A society with divorce rates above 40% really is not sustainable in the long run, I believe. The proposed solution is to restart a conversation about what marriage is and what the commitment means. I totally agree that this would help a lot. As a society, we should discuss and hopefully come to a conclusion that marriage is not just about love or adult desires, but is about the formation of families and providing for them a stable structure. However, it wouldn't work when people are using the 'what marriage really is' argument to exclude gay and lesbian people - again the important message would be lost in accusations of bigotry. A better way would be to allow gay and lesbian couples to get married as a matter of equal compassion and inclusion, which actually lets us then deal with the matter of what marriage is, without all the noise. Including gay and lesbian couples, who are by definition infertile couples, would not really distract from the idea of marriage being for procreation and for the stability of families resulting from the procreation act, any more than allowing heterosexual childless or infertile couples to marry (as we currently do) would. In reality, being rigid rarely works. I believe it would make perfect sense to say that marriage was meant to help couples set up family by encouraging procreation and then providing a stable structure for the resulting family, but being an inclusive society, we also extend this institution to cover those couples who unfortunately cannot procreate but are living in similarly committed arrangements.

The gay and lesbian couples seeking marriage and a family life, even if they do not have children to raise, are actively seeking to join the age old tradition of marriage and commitment. They have actively rejected the 'liberation' movement, which has promised them a life of endless hedonism, lots of sexual freedom and no institutions to rule their lives by. Just like us, they have chosen to reject the postmodern promise of endless freedom and have chosen to embrace instead the tradition of commitment and family values. Not many people out there are aware of this, but for choosing to side with tradition they often face the ridicule, disdain and outright discouragement of more 'liberation' orientated gay and lesbian people. For choosing to adopt our values and join our lifestyle, they have been derided as asssimilationists, people who are ashamed of who they are and seek conservative society's approval at all costs. We, the people who embrace family values, are their natural home. To reject them here too would be far too cruel and indeed inconsistent with our compassionate family values. To reject them would also be to confirm that their critics are right, that being gay means you cannot embrace family values, that you must embrace 'liberationism'. I really don't think that is the right message to send.

The fact that gay and lesbian couples are actively rejecting 'liberation' and embracing the tradition of marriage is another thing we should take heart to, and may even be able to use as a starting point for a general return to family values in society. The fact that gay and lesbian couples, who live in a culture where just a decade or so ago 'liberation' was the norm, have come to reject it so decisively, can be a great conversation starter for a wider societal discussion on marriage and family values, and why they represent a superior lifestyle to 'liberation'. Again, it is an opportunity we can only take if we first embrace the idea of marriage equality first.

Finally, many people, especially in the younger generations, are supportive of marriage equality as an idea. However, they are nowhere as passionate and committed as me in seeing this reform get done. The difference is because I believe in the essential conservative values of commitment, the importance of marriage, and the importance of family values for the future of our humanity, beliefs that have become too rare in our generation. Marriage equality will not fix all the problems surrounding marriage and family in our society, but it is where we must all begin. Sending the wrong message on this matter means not just that gay couples suffer - it gives a huge boost to our opponents in our long running battle for hearts and minds. This is why marriage equality cannot wait - it is an urgent priority. Ten years down the track, we may have lost a very good opportunity to change things indeed.

I Will Never Support Any Church Same Sex Marriage Campaign

Recently I was giving a speech on the topic of marriage equality again. I was asked a question about churches and same sex marriages. What if one day there is a campaign urging churches to perform same sex marriages?

Firstly, I will be staunchly opposing any action via politics or courts to force churches to perform same sex marriages. I will not just be taking a neutral stance, I will be opposing that action. I am surely many fellow supporters of marriage equality in the law would also stand with me on this issue. Any attempt at interfering with religion via politics, government or courts is an affront to religious freedom and the separation of church and state, and will never, ever be something I can morally support. Not now, not in 100 years time.

How about a campaign by church members themselves that doesn't involve the government or the law? I would stay out of that, as being not a member of any particular church I don't think I should have a say on that at all. The church members should solve it themselves, applying their own reasoning of religion. The only thing I would say about such a campaign is that the outside world should, as part of their respect for the freedom and dignity of religion, stay out of the conversation too if they are not a member of the said church. I will again staunchly oppose any attempt to influence church definitions of marriage from the outside world by cultural pressure.

Committed Gay Couples Who Don't Prefer Marriage Should Be Respected. They Also Don't Defeat the Need for Marriage Equality.

Believe it or not, there are gay couples out there who actually believe that marriage is 'too straight' for them, and they don't wish to take part in it. Now the anti-equality people have snatched this up as a vindication of their belief that marriage is heterosexual only. In turn, some sections of the equality community have questioned the motives of those gay couples who don't want marriage.

Actually, those gay couples who believe that marriage is 'too straight' are not only free to do so, they have a point too. Marriage will always be 98% straight even with marriage equality, and changing from 100% to 98% doesn't change anything really. Marriage will stay a straight culture based institution. If they want a gay culture based institution they can have their own.

But how about forcing all gay couples away from marriage? Just because it's straight culture based, doesn't mean it should exclude gay people. Society operates at its best whenever its institutions try to accommodate minorities' aspirations too. Our popular culture is mainly made by and for straight people, but does not exclude gay people. Likewise, to exclude Asian people from a festival of European culture because they may taint it with their Asianness is a very racist idea. They are welcome to participate as long as they respect that it is a festival of European culture, not Asian culture. They would not be forced to join the Asian culture festival instead. Moreover, marriage itself already inherently has that flexibility and compassionate accommodation - marriage has historically often been about procreation, but infertile couples are not excluded, for example.

Some gay people like to have a culture of their own, but most gay people from my observations tend to want to join mainstream society, and would fully respect the predominantly heterosexual character of it, as long as they are also allowed to join. Heterosexual society should accommodate them, therefore, just like most gay bars and gay parades also welcome straight people.

The other issue is that marriage, as an unfortunate consequence of developments during Western history, is written into the law, so marriage discrimination is legal discrimination.

Therefore, even if some gay couples want a gay culture based institution for commitment rather than marriage, that doesn't defeat the need for marriage equality.

Marriage Will Never be Obsolete. Here's the Future.

You all know that I am in the business of fighting for marriage equality, and I am serious about it. Recently, somebody asked me: marriage will be obsolete anyway, why fight for it?

The truth is that, marriage will NEVER be obsolete, and I really don't want to see it become obsolete either. I believe almost all those fighting for marriage equality will see it the same way. This is why it is a meaningful fight for us.

But nowadays couples are not choosing marriage in increasing numbers right? 25% of children are already not born in marriages, right?

Marriage is but one way of permanent commitment, truth to be told. It is especially appealing to those in some religious faiths, and maybe less appealing to others. But it is here to stay. Other forms of permanent commitment include civil unions and domestic partnerships, other religious covenants, and cohabitation backed up by declaration of permanent commitment to friends and family, for example. Even within marriage, some people choose a 'biblical' marriage, others opt for a civil ceremony. More choice that lead to the same objectives is always better. That objective is permanent commitment, and one that we would like to see encouraged. That means encouraging marriage, for now and forever.

In the future, marriage won't be the only choice for permanent commitment, but an equally valid choice amongst others to achieve the same objective. Therefore, it will always be encouraged, and will always be relevant. Therefore, we need to fight for marriage equality, and ignore those who want instead the 'abolition of marriage'.

On Opposing the 'Civil Union Boycott' Movement

Recently I have seen gay couples who have decided to 'hold off everything' until they can legally marry in their home country. This seems to be the case especially in places like parts of Europe and Australia, where marriage equality is not yet reality but might soon be. However, I really don't agree with this. In my opinion, if you are ready to commit, you should commit by having a ceremony and drawing up legal connections. If you are not ready to commit, that's another matter, but if you are ready to commit, you should.

The legislation of marriage equality, although important, is a political affair. Having a formal ceremony and drawing up legal connections as much as possible are personal affairs. If one cannot register a legal marriage yet, there are still ways to live in commitment, in the same spirit that a marriage should be lived in. One can have a formal commitment ceremony and at the same time have either a civil union or registered partnership (where it is available) or at least draw up legal contracts and update their will (where civil unions are not available). One can, in the ceremony, announce to everyone their legal commitments, and their spiritual commitments to stay together to the exclusion of all others and for life. After all, a publicly declared legal and spiritual commitment with the intention that this commitment is exclusive and lifelong is what marriage is about. This is the core of the spirit that should be guiding marriages anyway, and couples interested in marriage can and should also live in this spirit even where legal marriage is unavailable to them.

Marriage, Procreation and Same Sex Marriages: Part 1

Some people have argued that, as marriage was clearly designed for procreation, same sex couples just do not belong in marriage. They also say that allowing same sex couples to marry will mean that marriage is redefined to be about the emotional needs of adults.

I agree that marriage was clearly designed for procreation and it isn't just about love. Therefore, I do not support the idea of 'freedom to marry', I only support 'marriage equality'. There is no absolute freedom to marry just anybody you like, and there should not be. But including same sex couples in marriage is not about this. Marriage is a specific institution, and it should be kept that way.

The core of marriage is about procreation, it is the reason marriage exists. However we do allow infertile couples to get married. Anti equality advocates argue that this is because they still 'resemble' the arrangement for procreation, a wishy-washy argument that may also apply to at least some gay couples, e.g. butch-femme couples, and may be even applied to all gay couples since all of them are in conjugal relationships. I would rather argue that we let infertile couples marry because we are a decent society, and do not wish to exclude infertile people from marriage, so we have decided that infertile couples who otherwise live in a marriage like commitment are allowed to be married, even when they cannot procreate. We have made this decision as a society because the cost of maintaining absolute purity regarding marriage and its roots in procreation are not worth the discriminatory outcome that would taint our society so badly. The same case can be clearly made too regarding same sex couples.

More importantly, including infertile couples in marriage has not affected the central idea that marriage is for procreation, making the 'cost' of such inclusion only technical, and the case for excluding them only palatable to ideological purists, and not to the majority of the population where practical outcomes matter most. This is because infertile couples are a minority, and extending inclusiveness to them does not affect the central idea of marriage. To believe that by including gay people, comprising 2% of the population, in marriage is going to change what marriage is, is a ridiculous proposition. To uphold ideological purity now is even more ridiculous, when it has already been lost by including infertile couples. Excluding a whole class of people from an important institution in society because of a characteristic they were born with clearly taints the conscience of our society, and is clearly not worth it when the benefits are only to maintain some ideological purity, that has already been lost anyway.

A related argument against same sex marriages is that heterosexual marriages are 'complementary' whilst homosexual relationships are not. However, it is the same argument as the one above, just without spelling out the specifics. I cannot see where all heterosexual marriages are complementary and gay relationships are not, except in the field of procreation. Again, in the field of procreation, infertile couples can be said to be not strictly 'complementary' in function again, at least in some cases (e.g. where there is no womb for creating offspring in the woman). Again, to insist that this 'complementary' idea be an absolute requirement of marriage in every case is just another form of ideological purity over practical outcomes, and pertaining to an ideological purity that has already been lost anyway.

Marriage, Procreation and Same Sex Marriages: Part 2

Regarding the argument over marriage, procreation and same sex marriages, I sometimes cannot help but wonder if the people arguing on this basis against same sex marriages are really angry at something else, and are unfortunately taking their anger out on marriage equality. In what I believe to be an unfortunate development, many people in society have really decided that marriage shouldn't be about procreation and family but should be about only love. This, however, started out in heterosexual society and has nothing to do with marriage equality.

A common theme around opposition to same sex marriages state that it is a redefinition of marriage, and the last time that happened was with no fault divorce, which has brought on the consequence of broken families. From this line or argument, it is not hard to infer that at least some of the opposition to marriage equality is based on a fear that marriage will be further taken to be not about procreation and family. However, one can support marriage equality in the same way they support infertile couples being able to enter into marriage, without taking away from the belief that marriage is about procreation, unless one is an ideological purist, which most of us are not and should not be in relation to social matters. I, for example, am principally opposed to the idea of unilateral divorce. I personally am only not opposed to unilateral no fault divorce as law now because I respect the majority opinion on this. I see unilateral divorce as undermining the family, and I am not going to apologize for this. No fault divorce is applied across the spectrum, and represents a core change in the meaning of marriage, perhaps the most radical change ever. Marriage equality, on the other hand, is about extending some decency and equality to a minority group, and does not represent a core change to marriage as I outlined previously in Part 1.

There is indeed a case to be made for re-opening the discussion of divorce. It won't be popular, and it sure is not one of my priorities to help it along at the moment, but there are indeed merits to re-opening this discussion. There is surely widespread discomfort with the consequences of no fault divorce, and I believe only a frank discussion will solve the problem. But blaming everything wrong with no fault divorce on 'gay marriage' is the coward's way out. It is unfortunately too often cowards who hate the consequences of no fault divorce on society yet would not discuss that in fear of backlash, who have used 'gay marriage' as a surrogate thing to attack instead. We must not give credit to these cowards, cowards who do not even dare to challenge what they really believe is wrong but instead use an oppressed minority as a scapegoat.

Why Marriage Equality Concludes a Movement

Marriage equality is the civil rights issue of our generation. And not just that - it is likely the LAST major equal rights movement. Gender equality has been achieved, in my opinion. There may be a lot of racism out there, but at least the laws of modern Western nations are not actively racist (like segregation in the US or the White Australia Policy). People are also no longer discriminated in law based on their religion. In recent years gay and lesbian rights have advanced, to the point where marriage equality is the only missing thing in many Western nations.

It is in this background that I have come to the conclusion that marriage equality isn't just the end of the struggle for gay legal rights, but a perfect end to the whole equal rights movement. Marriage equality may be much less challenging and impact a smaller population than some of the previous waves, but it will be our generation that will have finally achieved the equal rights dream. It will be for this that we will be remembered.

Of course, the eradication of cultural racism and homophobia, as well as general social justice and civil rights issues remain things that we need to continue to fight for in the long term. Whilst homophobia eradication seems quite successful in parts of Europe, racism appears much more deep rooted unfortunately. But that's a separate issue.

Marriage Equality Is Just That

Maybe it is the fact that many marriage equality campaigns focus on the 'love=marriage' aspect, but there is considerable confusion over just what is marriage equality, and we need to address that. It is PURELY about equal opportunity that we have to address this problem. As a society we uphold equal opportunity, not equal outcomes. Everyone should have an equal opportunity before the law, but not everyone will get the same outcome and it's okay. Some people choose not to marry or cannot find the right partner, but that's okay - they have/had the opportunity to just like everyone else. Now we know that gay and lesbian people really cannot form a proper intimate relationship with the opposite sex, the basic requirement for a marriage not just on paper but in the spirit of the institution. Hence heterosexual only marriage laws effectively deny them any opportunity to enter the institution. That is inequality in opportunity. The fact that some heterosexual people who have had the equal opportunity still don't get married is besides the point. It's really about equal opportunity rather than 'love'.

Now I want to address some people's weird idea that marriage equality is not 'equality' yet, or that it just serves as a slippery slope towards the destruction of marriage. Both views are two sides of the same coin in fact, and probably arise from the wrong belief that supporting marriage equality means that everyone in love should be able to get married. And I will address them in one go.

"But someone may want to marry their dog" - Civil marriage is part of the secular legal system. As the legal system is set up to deal with interactions between people, not other animals, it cannot and will not deal with anything like this. Animals are not legal persons and cannot enter into contracts for example. Hence nobody can marry their dog anymore than they can sign a contract with their dog or make a will in favour of their dog. Not now, not in 5000 years.

"But someone may want to marry their cousin" - Nobody is wired to be exclusively attracted to their cousin. Heterosexual men who want to marry their cousins for example are also attracted to other women, with whom they can have an intimate relationship with, with whom they can get married to and live a proper married life. They are not excluded from marriage simply because they cannot choose to marry their cousin, unlike gay and lesbian people, who are excluded from marriage because they cannot have an intimate relationship with the opposite sex. Furthermore, the ban on marrying your cousin should apply equally to heterosexual and homosexual people, in a further show of equality.

"But someone may want to marry three partners" - Marriage in the modern secular Western legal system can only accommodate two people. Otherwise there will be real inequality. For example, a monogamous married couple can get tax breaks applied to the 2 people concerned. If polygamous marriage were recognised, some people will get the same tax breaks applied to 3 or more people, which is clearly an unfair situation under our modern secular standards. Some religious states allow polygamous marriage and can make it work because the concept of fairness in their legal system is based on religious doctrines. But in a secular Western state this can never happen. Hence marriage equality REQUIRES the rejection of legally recognised polygamous 'marriages'. (In fact I think this should be a point actually made as part of citizenship education for new citizens so that they will not think it is ever possible for our laws to be amended to accommodate polygamous marriages.)

Polygamy, or polyamory as some modern Western practitioners of this idea like to call it, is also fundamentally a choice, unlike sexual orientation. I know of many married men who would otherwise like multiple sexual partners too, but chose the path of marital monogamy because they believe such an arrangement to be best for their family, and that family welfare should come before any personal sexual needs. I happen to completely agree with them here, and this I think is the spirit of marriage. Hence choosing 'polyamory' is clearly equivalent to rejecting marriage itself, and marriage will never be redefined to include something so opposite to what it is, like the definition of black cannot include white. The men that choose marriage despite their sexual appetite are also as a result able to fulfil the spirit of marriage, as whilst they would like more sexual partners, they can be properly intimate still when there is only one partner, as clearly everyone who can be intimate with more than one person can also be intimate with just one person, although it may not fulfil their sexual appetites adequately - but fulfilling sexual appetites is not what marriage is for anyway. Gay and lesbian people are also able to fulfil the spirit of marriage if they choose to, except the law is excluding them. They have not rejected marriage, the law has rejected them. As it currently stands, they can either have a proper intimate relationship with someone of the same sex but cannot enter marriage, or they can on paper 'marry' someone of the opposite sex but can never fulfil the spirit of the institution.

"Everyone is equal - to marry the opposite sex" - Let me make an analogy here. Imagine if an office job stated that you need to be over 5'9" to apply. There are no sex or racial requirements. Yet such an advertisement would likely be illegal, as the requirement to be 5'9" excludes most women, and also most men of certain races. Under Australian law, for example, this is called 'indirect discrimination'.

"Some heterosexual people cannot find the right partner either and never get married" - Let me make another analogy here. Imagine a job requiring a person be white and also have a master's degree. There are many white people without a master's degree and hence cannot apply, just like the black man with a master's degree. However, this would still constitute racial discrimination, and is clearly unacceptable. This is what 'equal opportunity' is all about.

As you can see, 1) marriage inequality is a REAL issue not a theoretical one dreamed up by activists and 2) to make things equal it ONLY requires the inclusion of same sex couples. It will NEVER require or encourage another agenda, not now, not ever. In fact, even interracial marriage was a separate issue - there was no 'inequality' there, just that it was inhumane and racist. Separate issues are argued on their separate merits, just like interracial marriage was won and marriage equality is being won right now. If somebody else wants to further change the definition of marriage, it will be up to them to argue their merits, and for the cases I listed above, they will clearly fail.

Sound changes to institutions based on good reasons will never automatically lead to unsound changes. After all, women have been able to vote for almost 100 years now, are children and animals also entitled to vote? The interracial marriage movement, whilst changing marriage law, NEVER led to the opening of the gates for polygamous marriage for example, because they are separate issues. The marriage equality movement also will NOT open the gates for them to come in and ride on our backs, not now, not ever.

Understanding the Implications

Ten years ago, I could not say I was totally on board with gay equality as much as I can say that now. However, this year (March specifically) marks the 10th anniversary of me actively supporting marriage equality (then simply called same-sex marriage rights). My initial support of marriage equality came from a perspective of social libertarianism, inspired by the implications of the post-911 policies of conservative administration. At that time I was angered by the decision of Blair and Howard to enter the war on Iraq, even though a clear majority of their nations simply do not agree. 'Not in my name, not with my taxes' was a standard protest slogan.

Ten years later, marriage equality has long become a number one priority for me at the ballot box and elsewhere. At this time I am now angered by politicians including some here in Australia to block equality, even though a clear majority of their nations simply do not agree. 'Not in my name, not with my taxes' seems to apply equally well now.

A constant theme that we see is that we should not give too much power to governments on social matters. To let them regulate what society should and should not do, what values our nations should have etc. is simply dangerous.

How Many People are Affected by Marriage Equality?

Some people say that marriage equality will not benefit a lot of people. I would completely disagree.

The simple thing is that, the calculations given by those people for the percentage of people affected by marriage equality is wrong. Some suppose that as 2% of the population is gay and most are not in a hurry to get married, the issue affects less than 1% of the population. But my take is different. As it is basically an issue of dignity, equality and human rights, it affects the whole 2%+ of the LGBTI community, interested in marriage or not. And then it also affects their family and friends, so you have to times that by a few fold at least. Therefore, marriage equality benefits around 20% of the population roughly, in my opinion.

I'd Rather Burn in Hell than Support Bigotry

Conservative Christians have said that people who support gay marriages will burn in hell. Well, I am not a conservative or a Christian, but let's suppose that's true. I still would support marriage equality. I just cannot bring myself to do otherwise.